Bandit Country

Seven days in the life of a British Solider

RIP - Jim Hutton: 16th April 1949 – 27th October 2020
40th Field Regiment Royal Artillery

Geoffrey McMullan

Published by

Pathfinder-UK

6 Tray Lane, Atherington, Umberleigh,
Devon, EX37 9HY
United Kingdom

E-mail: geoffrey@macmullan.plus.com
Web: www.pathfinder-uk.com

First Edition Copyright © 12th July 2020
Geoffrey McMullan BEM - All rights reserved.

ISBN: 978-0-9576181-6-9

No part of this book can be reproduced in any form or by written, electronic or mechanical, including photocopying, recording, or by any information retrieval system without written permission in writing by the author. Although every precaution has been taken in the preparation of this book, the publisher and author assume no responsibility for errors or omissions. Neither is any liability assumed for damages resulting from the use of the information contained herein. Some of the facts have been slightly distorted to protect operational matters.

In memory of all those who
lost their lives during the troubles.
May you rest in peace.

Advanced Reviews

"The authors voice comes through strongly in his telling of a time spent crawling around and hiding under bushes. Anyone who knows the author will recognise his accent and intonation in the authentic telling of this adventure. I loved the interweaving of his own jeopardy with that of the natural world he was so intimately attempting to melt into. A good story well told of what in retrospect is an entertaining, informative, and gripping episode."

Dr Stephan Natynczuk – UK

"Tonight I read Bandit Country and felt like a man at a meal who has discovered his appetite. The starter was everything I expected when Geoffrey McMullan was the chef and even more to boot. I read it from start to finish and could not believe I had got to the end of the meal. I was left wanting more than I received. To me this novelette was a starter and I now want the meal, so Geoffrey had better get back to the keyboard and start meeting expectations as I guarantee whoever reads this will want to know much more of what Geoffrey has to share. A great first part of what promises to be a fascinating set of military memoirs covering his years in the military."

Jamie C McCready - UK

"Bandit Country is a masterfully written short read by Geoffrey McMullan, BEM, with a big bang! This short story fully engages the reader right from the start, as the story unfolds and reveals the very inner sole of a soldier out on a mission – one that could ultimately end in life or death. While the common bystander may observe a soldier exploring, say, a countryside landscape, much more than the eye can see is really at stake. With carefully planned and well thought out manoeuvres, a soldier is often actually risking his life for the sake of his mates and his Country. Like a wild animal, he must be fully aware of his surroundings and any cues or changes that could be a warning of danger. Through tracking, keen observations, and shifts in the local wildlife behaviour, a keen sense of awareness ultimately leads the main character in this story to a point of success. Sacrifices, teamwork, and inner strength are a must for such missions. The author does the world a great service with this eye-opening read bringing to light that soldiers are not just pieces on a chessboard, but rather real people, with real emotions that must be carefully kept in check in order for a mission to succeed. This is a must read once started, one will not want to put it down."

Vicky Burke -Conservationist - USA

"I have just finished reading this book which, in the preface, is described as a fictional story. It has real life events woven into the storyline and does give a refreshing insight into the day-to-day duties' soldiers serving in Northern Ireland endured. It makes a pleasant change from reading those stories embedded in Politics and Religion with anger and disagreement at the heart. The preface states that "The story attempts to take no political, religious or ideological viewpoint; it only aims to express some of the thoughts and emotions of an individual's stance of the situation in which he finds himself." In my opinion the book is successful in this statement, as it challenges what the layman's view might be of a serving soldier, in the army, in Northern Ireland during the troubles. A soldier as a hard, unthinking, unfeeling, military machine just doing what they are told to do by their superiors and the government. The way this story is written, you realise that, even with the training, sense of duty and honour, this soldier is deep, emotionally observant, close to nature and certainly a moral and spiritual individual. This is borne out by the detailed descriptions of sounds, surroundings, nature, and birds that the writer includes in his content. The time spent to set the scene and paint a picture in words, that you can visualise, is well worth it. The writer's knowledge of nature, animals, birds and especially his surroundings adds to the atmosphere of the story and certainly seemed to help keep him one step ahead, which was important to his own, and fellow soldiers' survival. The first chapter is a prime example of this and ends "……and just one unguarded moment could…. COST US OUR LIVES." The story describes how decisions were made to observe 'The Bandits' and keep them under surveillance using deep cover. The detail used to describe COP and the whole process getting there safely, makes the story compelling and real. You can almost imagine, moving along the pathways, getting through the bushes, and avoiding detection at all points. Immediate, life or death choices as a team bringing home the levels of stress and concern not only for yourself but your mates. Hearing a blackbird calling out, knowing the sound and that it was warning of approaching people or an animal. Time to get into cover!! Observing the ground, "Interestingly, footprints can give you more information than a fingerprint." Read on you will find out how, it's fascinating!! This is a short but compelling read, that is easy to pick up but leads you to the end without putting it down! It is enlightening and insightful. The glossary helps to understand the terminology used in the story and is worth looking at before you start. I highly recommend this book, as it may lead to a change in your own impressions of military personnel and process, which is something most people find hard to comprehend!!"

Geoff Dunsmore - UK

"Geoffrey McMullan's Bandit Country puts you inside the mind and skin of a British soldier on patrol for seven days in Northern Ireland during the Troubles. His eye for detail, down to the significance of dewy grass and bird calls, gives a realistic sense of place with all the sounds, smells, sweat, and suspense of patrol along with a dash of fear and a fascinating dose of tracker insight. This is an authentic addition to the genre of British soldier memoirs. It pulled me in, and I found myself wondering what was coming next."

Tim Pearson – USA

"I was completely engaged in Bandit Country from the first chapter. It describes a man's direct experience of day-to-day life in the extraordinary conditions of a serving soldier in Northern Ireland. There are insights into the practical challenges of existing in a hostile environment and the constant pressure that it imposes. It brings a soldier to life as a normal human-being, being asked to negotiate extreme circumstances. Bandit Country also gives hints to the power of observing and understanding nature - something Geoffrey gives more air to in his other range of books and the courses he runs. A very enjoyable read."

Barry Smale - Psychotherapist and Chi Kung Teacher

"As an Ex-Soldier who has completed multiple tours serving in a hostile environment that was Northern Ireland. I can honestly say that this book approaches the troubles from a different perspective. It is a great read for people who have never served and seek to have a greater understanding of what it means to be a British Soldier. The book is not full of military jargon or fire fights and it takes away the image of the perceived norm of a programmed thug that only follows orders and cannot think for himself or outside the box. Soldiers only have 5 or 6 seconds to react to a hostile situation and to make a life-or-death decision and all of this is over and above of what we consider to be a normal life…"

Maurice Newell – Retired British Solder

Glossary

1. **Yellow Card:** Printed on yellow card the British Army had rules of engagement which soldiers were expected to abide by and dictated when they could use their weapon.
2. **IRA:** Irish Republican Army: A paramilitary organisation. In that part of the world by 1977 there would have been no Official IRA.
3. **Dead Ground:** Is an area of ground hidden from an observer due to undulations in the land.
4. **Players:** British Army slang for members of a paramilitary organisation.
5. **Cache:** Means (that) bomb-making equipment/weapons have been hidden or stored away, to be retrieved at a later date.
6. **Quartermaster:** Was the person who arranged for the weapons and equipment that the IRA needed to carry out their attacks.
7. **COP:** Covert Observation Post.
8. **Tout:** In Ireland, a tout is an informant, or a super-grass.
9. **Dicked:** Is a term given to IRA lookouts. Unarmed and very junior. They are low grade; reporting on troop movements and other intel considered useful to the IRA. It was a way for someone to enter the paramilitary world.
10. **Provos:** Another name for the Provisional Irish Republican Army.
11. **Brick:** This was an adaptation of the older military formation where soldiers would form up as a square.
12. **HQ:** Headquarters.

13. **Barrett M90 . 50:** The Barrett M90 is a bolt-action, bullpup sniper rifle chambered in .50 BMG (12.7×99mm NATO).
14. **Comms:** Communications.
15. **Rat Pack:** A standard British Army ration pack has around 3500 Kcal. A 24-hour pack is designed to provide enough food Kcal for a full day of heavy-duty activities.
16. **Pigged out:** To fill up on food.
17. **VIP:** Very Important Paper = Toilet paper.
18. **VCP:** Vehicle Check Point.
19. **TAB:** Tactical Advance to Battle. 'Tabbing' is a physical exercise unique to the military. It prepares soldiers for carrying heavy equipment over long distances within a certain time frame.
20. **NVG:** Night Vision Goggles is a device that allows images to be produced in levels of light approaching total darkness.
21. **SLR:** The L1A1 Self-Loading Rifle, capable of firing NATO 7.62 ammunition.
22. **Tail-end-Charlie:** British slang from WWII, meaning the last aircraft in a formation, the man guarding the rear of a patrol or the rear gunner in a bomber.
23. **IED:** Improvised Explosive Device.
24. **Line Abreast:** A formation in which a number of soldiers travel side by side as a single unit, for example crossing a road/track. This reduces the chances of coming under fire.
25. **DLB:** A dead-letter box is a way of passing information between two parties, by using a secret location. By avoiding direct meetings, operational security is maintained.
26. **Ghost Walked:** This is a long-established way of walking quietly for the British Army. The technique allows you to

feel the ground slowly/gently with your foot to avoid snapping sticks etc, in order to minimise noise.
27. **All Round Defence:** Is a defensive fighting position that gives military units an ability to repel an attack from any direction.
28. **Face Veil:** A meshed cloth used as a scarf intended for personal camouflage. When draped over the head, you can see through it whilst concealing your face, or when tied over equipment, it breaks up the outline and reduces shine.
29. **Bumped:** Is when the enemy carry out a surprise attack.
30. **PIRA:** Provisional Irish Republican Army is a paramilitary organisation.
31. **Rear Party:** Soldiers on rear party are left behind while the rest of the regiment are deployed to a conflict zone. They are charged with the day to day running of the camp and its security.
32. **Riding Shotgun:** This is when you are giving covering fire from the rear of the vehicle.
33. **P-Check:** This is a 'personality' check.
34. **Tin City:** Originally built from corrugated sheets; eventually becoming a fully mocked-up village used for urban warfare training at first for Northern Ireland training and later for other conflict zones around the world.
35. **Int Sec:** The Intelligence Section collates information in an attempt to build a bigger picture of what the IRA might be planning. No amount of info is considered too small.
36. **Winthrop's Theory:** Also known as Winthropping is a cache finding technique. Developed by Captain Winthrop, he created a list of key analytical features greatly increasing the chances of finding weapons/bomb making equipment.

37. **Buddy, Buddy System:** An example of this is if someone went down with hypothermia, he would be stripped, put into a sleeping bag and another soldier (his buddy) would do the same. It was a way of helping to warm him up by transferring body heat. Used in extreme environments.
38. **Stand To:** British Army slang; meaning an attack is imminent, troops needed to get to their firing positions ready to repel an enemy attack.
39. **Bug Out:** To leave quickly if you are about to be overrun by enemy forces.
40. **Burst Transmission:** Is a compressed message sent at a high data signalling rate within a short transmission time.
41. **VRN:** Vehicle Registration Number or number plate.
42. **Bergen:** Originally an A - Frame rucksack designed by a Norwegian called Ole F Bergan. Through time the name shifted to Bergen.
43. **Sod's Law:** is a British culture axiom that "if something can go wrong, it will", and it will happen at "the worst possible time" This term is commonly used in the United Kingdom, in North America "Murphy's law" is more popular.
44. **Flagging:** Is when plants are compressed under the weight of someone, indicating their direction of travel.
45. **True-Track:** The actual track.

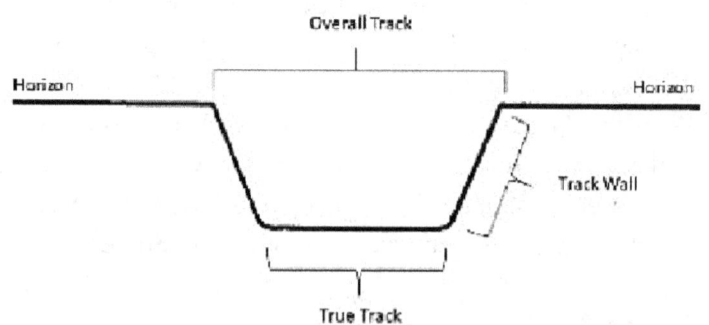

46. **Estimating height of an individual (Pax):**

Pax	Foot Length in Inches	Multiply by	Divide by	Approximate Height in Inches	Divide by	Height in Feet & Inches
1	11.5	100	15	77	12	6.3
2	10.5	100	15	70	12	5.8

47. **Hot Pursuit:** This refers to the urgent and direct pursuit of a suspect by military forces.
48. **Backtrack:** This is when someone attempts to step in their own tracks while moving backwards. They will always leave an extra footprint over the top of their first print. This is an indication of someone attempting to backtrack.

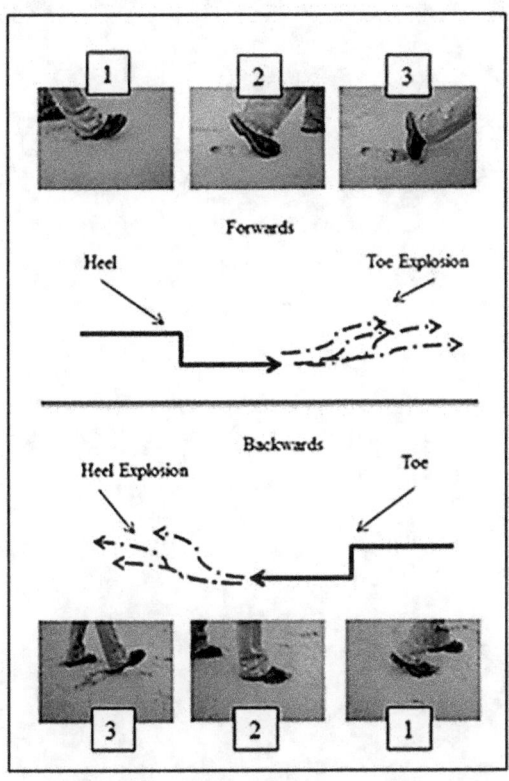

49. **Fouled:** A track placed over another track making it difficult to see the first track is considered a fouled track.
50. **ASU:** Active Service Unit.
51. **Gardaí:** The police service of the Republic of Ireland.
52. **HLZ:** Helicopter Landing Zone.
53. **IA:** Immediate Action: Something that needs to be done before anything else: like put the kettle on for a brew.

Contents

	Glossary	11
	Preface	19
Chapter 1	Two Worlds	21
Chapter 2	Hostile Country	25
Chapter 3	Going to Ground	31
Chapter 4	Reflections	39
Chapter 5	Stand To	47
Chapter 6	The Hunt	51
Chapter 7	End of Mission	57
	The Author	61
	Acknowledgements	62

Preface

This fictional story is not about blood and guts. However, it does include some real events that have been woven into the storyline; the intention is to take you on a short journey of some of what a British Soldier might go through on a tour of Northern Ireland (N.I.) in 1977, known as 'Operation Banner'. It is about seven days in the life of one individual human being who has been thrust into an environment of intense pressure: a place where the difference between right and wrong hangs in the balance. The threats he faces require split-second decision making, which rest solely with him and are based on the rules of engagement known as the Yellow Card[1], which he is duty bound to uphold. The story attempts to take no political, religious, or ideological viewpoint; it only aims to express some of the thoughts, and emotions of an individual's stance on the situation in which he finds himself. The story touches on some of the *known* tactics used by the IRA[2] and what it might have done for the British Soldier's skill base. While tracking and nature awareness, may not have been common place in the British Army at that time, soldiers were certainly engaged in urban tracking; while rural tracking was an aspect that some would have engaged in, from individuals to Special Forces.

All views expressed are solely for the purpose of the story and are not intended to be an authority on N.I. and should not be considered as such. The characters are fictional. Many people will have different views given the complicated nature of what became known as...

THE TROUBLES

Chapter 1

Two Worlds

I awoke to the sound of the dawn chorus. I was enjoying the warmth of the sun as it gradually drove the chill from my bones. There was a fresh breeze passing over my face. In silence, I watched and listened to the long grass as it continually changed direction; swirling around as it danced with the wind. I felt as if I had not a care in the world, as I enjoyed what nature had to offer me; I could hear Chaffinches calling and a Blackbird singing from a tree to my right, a distant Yellowhammer announced its presence, with its distinct 'a-little-bit-of-bread-with-no-cheese' call. In the valley, there was a small farm, the smell of which had reached my nostrils transporting me back to my childhood. I recalled playing with my friends in the woods and fields; my dad used to fly his pigeons in the very same fields that bordered the back of our house.

    I heard muffled voices coming from the farm, that is when I became aware of a Hooded Crow flying across the field in front of me. It was coming from the direction of the farm. I watched as it passed over some dead ground[3]; when it dipped briefly before resuming its original course. Something or someone was in the dead ground; I focused in on the area where the crow had dipped. Moments later, a stunning Red Fox came into view; first, the head appeared, followed by the rest of the fox. It was a vixen; her coat was shining beautifully in the morning light. I watched as she cautiously slipped away quietly sniffing the air as she went, eventually disappearing from view.

    I guess she had been out looking for food, maybe even a mate. As a birdwatcher I had learnt that birds can tell us what is going on in the neighbourhood; the crow dipping was one of those signs, and by now all the other wildlife would be aware of the vixen's presence, either from the alarm calls or, maybe they had seen the crow dipping; either way, they would understand the signals that were being sent out. I could not hear if the crow called out or not, as the wind drowned out any sound from reaching my ears. As I lay there, I thought about what the birds might be saying to each other or indeed to us.

When they are alarmed, no translation is needed. Once I realised it was a fox and not a human, I relaxed. She seemed unaware of us hiding in the shadows; reassuring me that the wind was masking our presence or that, not having washed in days we were smelling like our surroundings. As long as the birds were not alarming over our presence, I felt that we were safe. If anyone were watching the area, hopefully they would be unaware of our presence as well. I laid back looking skyward; I was trying to locate the Skylark that was singing its heart out above me. It was not long until I spotted it. Like the smell of a perfume that reminds you of your favourite aunty; this little bird reminds me that spring has arrived.

Sometimes, I would fall asleep listening to its beautiful song; but not today: today or any day soon was not a good time to doze off. I felt a gentle squeeze of my foot. Turning I saw Peter slowly and quietly moving over, allowing me to take a look at what he was pointing at. It was a car parked up by the farmhouse, it drove off slowly down the road, briefly stopping a couple of times before moving off again. I wondered if this could be the players[4] tasked with collecting the contents of the cache[5]. It used to be that the IRA Quartermasters[6] house would be located close to where the cache was hidden. I was in a place of two worlds, one being nature and the other was an operational tour in my own country as a British Soldier in Northern Ireland. I was part of a COP[7,] my team consisted of Taff, Jock, Peter, and myself (a Belfast Boy). In situations like this, fear could set in.

Having said that I always viewed fear as a positive thing. When I feel fear, I know I am alive, all my senses and skills go into overdrive. Fear seems to slow time down; allowing you to respond to events happening on the ground in a split second. We knew we were up against hardcore players and just one unguarded moment could:

Cost us our lives...

Chapter 2

Hostile Country

We were only a few miles from the border with Southern Ireland (Eire), in what is known as bandit country. This was an extremely hostile environment to be in; more British Soldiers lost their lives in this area compared to any other part of N.I.

***

Acting on a tip-off from a tout[8], a search team was deployed to an old derelict house on the outskirts of town; I say derelict because it was nothing more than a pile of rubble; our mission was to locate the whereabouts of a cache of arms/explosives. I was part of the cordon assigned to protect the search team. A short while into the search, I spotted a naked plastic doll; that was nailed at eye level to a tree that stood close to the derelict property. The doll was about four inches in size; I stood with my back to it and looked out across the countryside. In the distance, stood a large lone oak tree on top of a hill, in front of it was a hedgerow which bordered the field opposite from where I was standing. Along the front of and close to the hedgerow was a group of around seven exceptionally large well-established gorse bushes; many more were scattered throughout the undulating field; some even intermingled with other hedgerows and stone walls. An animal trail led away from a wooden gate on the opposite side of the road from where I was standing; I followed it with my eyes as it weaved its way up the field to a gap in the hedgerow, passing to the right of the large gorse bushes.

Having made the search team aware of the doll and of the oak tree in the distance (which could be considered a primary marker leading to a possible cache), two patrols were tasked to carry out a sweeping search of the area.

The patrols were careful not to head straight for the oak just in case we were being Dicked[9]. This would be a safe bet as the Provos[10] always watched over their caches, making sure they were not found. The patrol was looking for markers that would lead them to the cache. These markers needed to be natural objects that stood out from the rest of the surroundings, but not too obvious or there would be no point in hiding the cache. The instructions on how to locate the cache had to be clear and simple; so that those collecting the contents would be able to find it with ease and speed in an area that may be unfamiliar to them.

Eventually, one of the patrols reached the oak tree; assuming that it was the primary marker the Brick[11] Commander stood near it. He, along with the rest of the patrol scanned the area until they spotted what looked like secondary markers, these led to a small burnt-out gorse bush, which was located behind a stone wall in dead ground. From where he was standing it was in direct line of sight to the doll nailed to the tree, but the burnt bush could not be seen from the doll. Investigating the only burnt-out bush in the whole area, the patrol commander saw that the topsoil had been disturbed next to it, removing the top soil he discovered a buried milk churn. Removing the lid, he found a disassembled rifle wrapped in hessian cloth.

He reported the find, he received orders that the patrols were to continue to carry out a search of the rest of surrounding area; hopefully giving the impression that the cache had not been found. They continued the search and slowly made their way back to their vehicles. On hearing this news, I had a real sense of achievement; I had been part of a process that led to discovering a weapon, which was to be used to harm or kill a British Soldier.

It was quickly decided to send my Brick in, to set up a covert observation post, in order to keep the cache under surveillance. It felt really good to be an active part of what I hoped would be the arrest of a sniper and the saving of a life.

We were tasked with monitoring all movements, looking for patterns made by the locals whether on foot or in a vehicle and informing HQ[12] when the weapon had been picked up. HQ would then task the follow-up teams to track the men that collected the weapon; in the process they were to identify all the players within the chain from the cache to the shooter. I say shooter; more like sniper because the cache contained a Barrett M90 .50[13] calibre sniper rifle. Finally, we were tasked to backtrack the individuals who dropped the weapon off and to establish where they crossed the border and to look for signs of it being used as a regular crossing point from the south into the north.

***

With a strong sense of excitement, we quickly put our kit together, preparing ourselves for a long-protracted period of surveillance. Radios were checked and comms[14] established with the control station 'callsign Zero'. Our medical kit and our Rat Packs[15] were packed away. We had to eat our food cold; we could not cook it because the smell would attract unwanted attention. Instead, we pigged-out[16] in the cookhouse before deploying. Our water bottles were filled, and small black bin liners were packed, we used these to defecate in.

Plastic bottles were used to piss in; and to contain our smell from any animals that may be drawn by our scent. The bottles were always checked thoroughly to ensure they would not leak and were safe to use, as they were later transported back to camp in our backpacks. It was of the utmost importance that they were packed in a way that they would not get damaged. Last but not least you packed your VIP[17].

***

Our routes in and out were plotted; making sure we did not use the same route twice. We logged and confirmed our extraction point, which would be implemented when 'Zero' received the code word 'Triangle' from me over the radio. It was done this way to reduce the exposure time for the RAF helicopter to be in the air, as the IRA were very keen to shoot one down.

This would be a massive morale booster for them as they would be sending a strong message to us that we were not safe even in the air. Weapons and ammo checked; we also made sure that nothing on our person would give us away, either by sound or shine, reducing our chances of being seen or heard by the locals, who would give us away to the Provos.

We applied camouflage cream to reduce any shine, and any loose items were either secured or removed if not needed. We knew that if we got spotted the IRA could set up an ambush within twenty-five minutes, ready to engage us in a firefight. It was vital we did everything to reduce the risk to our safety. We were about to deploy to our drop off point when Peter called out; "has anyone got the secateurs?"; we looked at each other with blank expressions: shit, we nearly forgot a vital piece of equipment!

***

While we waited for the secateurs to arrive, Jock decided to share a story from his last tour in bandit country. He told us that he had stopped a car with a single occupant in order to carry out a vehicle check. The lady driver rolled down her car window and said, we do not see many soldiers in these parts, to which Jock replied, I fail to see why not, there are patrols all along the border madam. She smiled and said that may be, but we are in Southern Ireland. Jock said that he felt panic set in as he realised that they had crossed the border by some three hundred metres. They chatted for a while ending with smiles and hugs all round, before legging it back over the border sharpish, preventing a major incident with the Republic.

***

It was now time to go; we tagged onto a multiple foot patrol and headed out with them to set up a VCP[18], which lasted no longer than twelve minutes; due to the speed, the Provos could deploy gunmen to our area of operation.

Under the cover of darkness, while the other teams carried out the vehicle checks, we slipped into the shadows, dropping down into a tree-covered ditch with heavy undergrowth. Our objective was some three miles away; we travelled lightly in order to cover ground quickly, and if need be to effect a fast escape in the event we got compromised; after all; we were in…

Bandit Country…

Chapter 3

Going to Ground

The ditch afforded us excellent cover, effectively screening us from the full moon and anyone who might be watching out for army patrols. Having exhausted all the cover that was available to us; we broke out into a small field that undulated greatly. It was bordered on one side by a hedgerow on a high mound that cast long shadows over the field. Both of these helped to screen our movements as we tabbed[19] to our objective.

***

I looked up the hill to our right: it would have been quicker for us to go up and over it. However, it would have been a risky thing to do. As we would have crested going over the top of the hill, even laying down and rolling over the top, for a brief moment, we would have stood out in the fullness of the moonlight which lit up the surrounding countryside.

I loved being in nature especially at night; it felt quite different to our daytime patrols. There were fewer distractions at night, giving you a greater sense of being connected to and somewhat in control of your environment.

We continued to stay in the shadows, avoiding open ground as much as possible. The route we were on was the best option, even if it did take us longer to reach our objective. We made several stops in order to survey the surrounding area for any suspicious movement. We listened and watched; trying to pick out any sign that we were being observed; we also had the advantage of our NVG[20] which allowed us to see better in the dark. Objects which appeared dark were highlighted by a bright green light.

***

A gentle wind brought with it the sound of rustling leaves as they rolled past me. In the distance I could hear a fox call, sadly, there were no Tawny Owls calling; they never made it as far as Ireland; for me, they would have been the icing on the cake. I gently tapped the magazine of my SLR[21] indicating we were about to move. As we moved off, I looked behind me to check that our Tail-end Charlie[22] was with us, because he was at the rear, he would be mostly looking away from us, and he might have missed hearing me tap my magazine.

***

After several hours we approached an iron gate which led onto a small backroad; on the opposite side of the road was a similar gate. Both were potential danger points for an ambush or the placing of an IED[23]. Taking cover and adopting a prone position, we waited for a while. We surveyed the area for signs of trouble. The ground was soft underfoot, and the tread from our boots was clear for all to see.

We took the opportunity to change into our blacked-out trainers. While one person changed the others took up defensive positions. The idea behind the switch was to further reduce the risk of being discovered as we approached our objective; military boot prints would be a dead giveaway to the locals that soldiers were in the vicinity; increasing our chances of being engaged in a firefight.

We spotted several openings in the hedge to our right; these were good places to get through the hedge, but also perfect for an IED. People, like animals, tend to take the path of least resistance and the Provos would be banking on us being complacent. We decided to go to the left of our position; the hedge there had no gaps, so the chances of encountering an IED were slim, besides, we had our own way of getting through the hedge.

As we approached the hedge; we found a dip in the ground; we crawled into it, meant that we were less exposed, it provided us with a small degree of protection. Taff got out the secateurs and began to cut low under the hedge creating a gap big enough for us and our kit to pass through the thorny hawthorn hole that Taff had created. Last man through replaced the cut-offs plugging the gap and covering the white ends of the cut branches with dirt so as not to draw attention to our presence.

The hedgerow was constructed on an earth bank which resulted in a corresponding linear ditch which ran parallel to the base of the bank. At the bottom of the ditch was a small stream. We slipped down into the roadside ditch avoiding the water so as not to leave wet foot prints on the road surface when we crossed it. We waited and once we were satisfied it was safe to cross, we moved line-abreast[24]; once over, again we waited to ensure we had not been seen. You can imagine four men leaving wet foot prints in a line, a most unusual sight, and a dead giveaway. It was on this side that we needed to establish a DLB[25] just in case; our comms went down.

We found the ideal place just to the right of the gate. Messages from us or headquarters would be secreted under a large stone, which was immediately in front of a speed sign. The location of which was transmitted to 'Zero'. We had regular check-ins on the radio; if our comms failed; we switched to using the DLB.

Having established that it was safe, we cut our way through the next hedge on this side. Once through we moved off and re-joined the track thirty metres further along from the second gate.

***

Five hundred metres from our objective, we slowed down, so as not to disturb any wildlife. It is movement that will nearly always give you away: Think of our Kingfisher, a small bird with an iridescent turquoise blue body, a bright orange breast with a white head and throat markings; with such colours, you would think it would be easy to spot. Not so, not if it stays perfectly still, as soon as it moves, you see it and we did not want to announce our presence in the area.

We left the track and entered a small wood staying just beyond the reach of the moonlight. Suddenly, Jock who was on point, stopped and gave the hand signal to get down on the ground. I sidled up to him to find out what the problem was.

He pointed ahead of us at a dark shape; it looked like someone was lying in wait. We froze for an extended period; I was concerned that we had been seen and we were about to walk into an ambush. The hairs on the back of my neck stood up, and my body was tingling, cold sweat trickled down my face. After some considerable time, I decided to approach slowly, only to realise that we had been shitting ourselves over what turned out to be an old log. With a sense of relief, we continued. The sound of leaves being gently crushed underfoot reached my ears, as we slowly ghost walked[26], being careful not to snap any twigs with our weight.

***

I caught the smell of a wood-burning fire and I knew that we were getting close to where we needed to be. The smell was coming from the only farmhouse for miles around. After leaving the wood, we moved slowly up the track until we reached the gap in the hedge that I had seen from the derelict house earlier that day.

There was another opening further along, which was big enough for heavy farm equipment to pass through; there were tracks indicating that the entrance had recently been used. The likelihood of it being booby-trapped was remote; nonetheless, we took no chances and checked it carefully for tripwires and sign of pressure plates.

***

The process of setting up in our chosen gorse bush was going to be slow; the whole time we had to be aware of any disturbance we might cause. We placed a thick piece of hessian on the ground in an attempt to reduce any sign we might leave. However, no matter what you do, you will always leave sign. The trick is to make it look as natural as possible, with our weight on the hessian it might be possible to confuse the flattened grass as somewhere an animal rested, such as a deer. The entrance to our COP was shielded from behind by several other large gorse bushes, which we had to negotiate before going to ground inside ours. All this had to be done with the knowledge that a player would be watching over the cache, making our movements very deliberate and slow. Peter reached in deep with the secateurs and started making cuts; just as before we needed to reduce the potential for any sign that would give us away. The rest of us went into all-round defence[27]

***

Once inside, movement was limited, even though we had cut away at the inside to make some room for us. Our observation window was low down, to see it from the outside a person would need to get down on the ground, it was difficult to see due to the overhang from the gorse. We were afforded good views of the track to our left and over to the cache area, as the field gently sloped away from us; we could make out the top of the burnt gorse bush. The IRA nearly always made sure that the approach to and from their caches were shielded from view so that they would not be detected.

To a similar degree, we needed to ensure that any light reflected from our sights or binoculars would not give away our position. As well as the overhang, to help prevent any shine we draped our face veils[28] over our optics. We plugged the gap behind us with the offcuts, ensuring that it looked as natural as possible, this included running a hand over the grass at the entrance to encourage it to stand back up, having been flattened by our weight.

We took up our positions: From being the observer to the sentry and because the space was tight it was necessary to sleep back-to-back. One would relax while the other slept. In such a confined space, you had to be comfortable with your mates tending to their personal needs. We used this time to change back into our boots. Routine established; we settled in; first light would be in a few hours.

***

I awoke to the sound of the:

Dawn Chorus...

Chapter 4

Reflections

We had been in our position for three days now. We maintained minimal movement staying as silent as possible and making sure we did not become complacent. This was of the utmost importance as the consequences were you could wind up dead.

Another unit lost several members of one of their COP teams. The poncho they had been using as a groundsheet had been flapping in the wind; and had been doing so for days. As they moved out of their position to return back to base, they got bumped[29]. The Provos had ambushed them; someone had seen the poncho flapping around and they fed that information back to the PIRA[30].

Carrying out surveillance also gives you time to reflect on events in your life from your family to work. I was constantly evaluating things, looking for ways of improving the skill base of my team and myself. The well-being of my men was uppermost in my thoughts. Jock's wife was about to have their first child. I was sure this would have been on his mind, that said he showed no sign of it; he was totally professional. As for me, even in conflict zones, I always found time to birdwatch on top of everything else and seeing the Hooded Crow was a great joy for me, as they did not occur where I lived.

Sometimes, I would role-play various scenarios in my mind; be it a robbery on a bus or a fight on a train. I would look at the possible outcomes for each situation and how I would deal with them; I still do it to this day. Doing this was way of keeping myself from going stir crazy.

Confined for days on end with three other men you needed to get on with them really well and I believe this helped us to get through living in such a confined environment.

***

At times, my thoughts were of home. I would not let these thoughts get in the way of doing my job. In my mind, my family were in another place that I would only go to it when it felt safe to do so. I also thought about the fact, that initially I was not allowed to deploy to Northern Ireland. I was told this was because I was from Belfast; as an Irishman you would normally be given a choice if you wanted to go or not. I was not given a choice, and this really pissed me off for several reasons.

As a soldier, even though you might be afraid you still wanted to know if you had what it takes to do your job, after all, that is what we trained for. Another reason was that I did not want to be left behind on rear party[31] especially while my buddies were in my country putting their lives on the line; for an extra £1.50 a day danger money before tax. Then there is the feeling, of being left out of their conversations when they returned. I also worried about how they might view me as an Irishman, having not been a part of what they would go through; would some of them resent me. I was determined not to be left behind; in my mind I was also concerned that I would no longer be a part of our family. I set out to do everything in my power to persuade my boss to let me go.

They said the reason for not being allowed to go was if I was recognised, my family were at risk of being taken hostage in order to blackmail me. As it turned out I was recognised while riding shotgun[32] on a mobile patrol. We were driving into Belfast from Aldergrove; the driver of a brown civilian Land Rover pulled up behind us at a set of traffic lights. He was calling out my name; in the moment I had no idea who this guy was; at the next set of lights I jumped out to P-Check[33] him. It turned out to be the son of my mum's best friend.

He, had never seen me with short hair, let alone in uniform. I certainly did not recognise him at first. Thank goodness nothing came of it and I reported the incident. Not being allowed to go may have even been due to the fact that I had been banned from Tin City[34] for being too violent. In the end, I was allowed to go; perhaps because I badgered my boss so much or due to the fact that we had lost a few guys during training; that the manpower levels dropped enough to allow me to go.

***

My passion for birds often made me the subject of piss-taking from the lads. I did not mind, as I saw it as a sign of affection; of course, when I pointed this out to them, they went Neanderthal on me and denied it, which provided me with a source of amusement.

I also have an interest in tracking animals; however, human tracking was and still is of particular interest to me. My inspiration for tracking came from a British Army tracker and survival expert Eddie McGee. North Yorkshire Police called for his expertise in helping them to track down a multiple murderer called Barry Prudom, also known as The Phantom in the Forest.

I gained an insight into tracking from Eddie's book 'No Need to Die' where he talked about tracking a guy in a desert region who was miles ahead of him; by simply following fly covered stones. As he travelled his quarry was sucking on dates for energy, and when he finished with one, he spat out the stone; there were traces of the fruits flesh left on each stone which attracted flies. This gave Eddie the sign he needed to track his quarry.

This bit of information lit something inside me and my tracking skills since then moved on leaps and bounds from Bob Carr an SAS tracker, to Tom Brown Jr at the Tracker School in the United States and my own personal experiences.

I had been introduced to tracking in real time while attending a Battlefield Survival course at the International Long-Range Reconnaissance Patrol School (ILRRPS); which was run by 22 SAS located in Weingarten in Southern Germany. I had considered joining 22 but decided against it as I had recently got married and we were about to have our first child. I also believed I did not have what it would take to be a member of 22.

***

While in our COP, I thought about the tactics the IRA employed. If you put aside religion and, ideology, I feel many soldiers might agree with me, that tactically the IRA was good for the British Soldier. When you think about the things they did and how they did them, it made them in part a formidable force to reckon with. Allow me to qualify this. In order to know your enemy; you need to think like them, you need to get inside their heads.

We were always told that no matter how small and irrelevant we think a piece of information might be, we still need to record it and pass it onto the Int Sec[35]. For example, while on an urban patrol, we knew that Mrs Smith at No. 32; normally has two bottles of gold top milk. However, one day there were two gold and three blue tops. No. 32 now becomes a suspect training house or a meeting place; either way it became a place of interest to us. A covert observation post would have been inserted to watch the comings and goings of No. 32 in order to establish if it really were a house of interest and not just family members paying a visit.

We also became aware that in another street all the door knockers had horses' heads except for one which had a dog's head, this could have been a possible safe house. Not far away in another street, all the gates were hinged on the left, again except for one which was hinged on the right; a possible escape route for a gunman/sniper. Many houses had painted the surrounds of their windows white so that at night a passing soldier would stand out as a potential target. There were no night lights back then that would light up the second someone passed by.

One time while on a mobile patrol, one of the lads went into a panic when he saw his name painted on the side of a building in large letters. It read, 'Brownly we are going to get you'. He thought it was him they were referring to this is like writing 'Smith we will get you', it is a common name. They were trying to mess with our heads and in his case it worked. Sometimes, when on patrol, you might come upon a group of kids playing football in the middle of the street; you hear a whistle, the kids run away, and a shot rings out, followed by another whistle and the kids run back into the road.

You cannot return fire for fear of shooting one of the children. They would hide bullets in the frames of bikes and get kids to deliver them to wherever or hide a bomb under someone's wheelchair. They have even been known to jack up a roof with a trolley jack so that a sniper can take a shot at a soldier and the list goes on. If you consider it from their perspective; they believed they were under occupation so you can kind of understand their actions. I am not in any way justifying their behaviour, just quietly admiring the ingenuity that they displayed. If the situation were reversed, would we not be using similar tactics if we believed we were being occupied by an oppressor?

We became just as ingenious; the lessons learned by the army in years to come will have stood British forces in good stead for dealing with insurgents in other worldwide conflicts.

Without going into detail, one good example of this was Winthrop's Theory[36]. As I said, the gathering of small bits of information and tip-offs from touts, allowed the Int Sec to build a bigger picture of what might be happening on the ground. At times they could see something was about to happen; they may not have known exactly what it might be. As a result, patrols would flood the streets in a given area. The sniper on seeing this might not take the shot, not if he believed his escape route was cut off increasing his chances of being caught. We may never know if this tactic was successful or not, we can only hope that lives were saved.

I would imagine a gunman making his escape after carrying out a shooting. He would run into the house with the dogs' head door knocker. Having changed his clothes, he headed out the back gate into one of the many alleyways that peppered Belfast and into the next house that might have a dog sign on the back gate. He would then walk out the front door of that house and head down the street of terraced houses. Arriving at the house where the gate is hinged on the right, ducking into it, he then walks through several houses that have had the interior walls knocked through. He heads out the back of the last house and walks down to the end of the alleyway, to be picked up by a waiting car.

There were also times when you passed a group of women, one of them would spit full in your face; sometimes they would drag phlegm up from the back of their throat and if her aim were good you got it full in the face. There seemed to be no end to the tactics they employed.

Then there was the physical side of things, being cooped up in a small space was extremely uncomfortable, being unable to stretch or walk about brought its own problems but none more so than the need to carry out your bodily functions. Due to the lack of room to move around in, it was necessary to use the buddy, buddy system[37]. This meant one of your team would have to hold the bin liner for you while you went about your business.

There was also a need to condition your body to urinate into a bottle at a different time to using the plastic bag. After you finished with the bag you placed inside a sealable plastic container: One to contain any possible leaks, and two to reduce the chances of the smell attracting unwanted guests be they animal or human.

N.I. was a steep learning curve...

Chapter 5

Stand To

It was five-thirty in the afternoon, when to our right, I spotted a small flock of birds take flight along the hedgerow which ran up from the farm. Someone or something was moving along the track on the other side of the hedge. Whatever it was, it flushed the birds and they exited from the hedge on our side. The birds hooked back behind whatever was causing the disturbance. It was like watching a Mexican wave as the birds responded to what was moving along the track indicating to me exactly where the perpetrator of the disturbance was.

***

In the distance, I could see a blackbird on top of a tree it was alarming while facing in the direction of the perceived threat. The Blackbirds alarm changes slightly in relation to the type of threat; by that I mean you can tell if the threat is human, dog, cat, or bird of prey. This led me to believe that there were indeed people moving along the track. I gently touched Peter's foot and indicated to him to stand to[38]. He alerted the others, before moving up to join me. Scanning the area Peter spotted a car parked up by the farm. We could see exhaust fumes rising up which meant that the engine was running. It was the same car that we spotted earlier on; they must have been checking the area out for patrols before committing themselves to collect the weapon. Any thoughts and feelings of home went to that other place to be replaced with the anticipation of a weapon about to be collected. Two men appeared by the gate, which was about halfway along the hedgerow, they paused and looked around before entering the field and heading straight for the cache.

When you are with your team for long enough you develop a special bond that needs no words, you just know what the other person is thinking and feeling, combined with your training everything falls into place. This bond continues even when you leave the army.

There are times when you do not get on with each other. However, regardless of your differences; you have each others' backs. These are men who would stand in the thick of it with you and you would stand in the fire with them. Without me saying a word Jock opened up the entrance to our COP in preparation for a quick bug out[39] and a possible firefight if need be. Should that happen, we would have to move fast, after issuing a warning order as per the Yellow Card. In effect, our COP had the potential to become an ambush as well. Our aim would be to capture them or if need be use deadly force. The latter was always my last choice, simply because to take a life regardless of ideology is a big thing to do. Nonetheless I was prepared to do it simply because they would not hesitate to take mine or my men's lives.

***

It was starting to get dark when we switched to our NVG. Once illuminated, the area showed up well as we watched them recover the weapon. Immediately they headed back to the gate and made their way down the track at pace. Once in their car, they drove off towards Belfast. Using a burst transmission[40] Taff sent descriptions of the men, the VRN[41], the type of car and direction of travel to HQ, informing them of the pickup. It was now up to the follow-up teams to stay with them and discover who else was involved and to discover the location they were heading for. If we were lucky, we would bag the sniper as well.

***

After all this excitement, we continued to lay up for a further twenty-four hours. We wanted to ensure that we would not get

Dicked by a local or an IRA observer. Grabbing a bite to eat from our cold rations we settled down into a normal night routine.

***

When packing your Bergen[42] you always made sure that the items you needed the most were at the top of your backpack and when you finished with them you immediately put them back into your Bergen and you secured the straps. In the event you had to bug out quickly, you would grab your Bergen and off you went. If you had not returned any items after using them, you had to leave them behind and Sods Law[43] says the item you left behind is the one you needed the most. This lesson is often learnt the hard way and never forgotten. Personal routine completed all we needed to do now was to conserve our energy for:

Tracking our Quarry...

Chapter 6

The Hunt

Wildlife is always very alert going into and from their dens. The last thing they want is to put their offspring at risk of being attacked. Just like them, this is when we are most at risk of being attacked and killed.

Just before first light we quietly and cautiously slipped out from our COP, which had been our home now for four days. We needed to get to the cache before dawn, so I could observe any dew on the ground which would indicate their direction of travel. Hopefully, any players that were watching over the cache had long gone by now, making it safe for us to track out of the aera. The weather was mild but damp; while I looked for their tracks the rest of the team went into all round defence just in case we got bumped.

We were in luck; they had left by the same route they had arrived from. This made tracking them easier as we had two sets of tracks in close proximity. If they had taken a different route out there was no guarantee that they would be heading for the border. In which case I would have tracked the original set of tracks coming from the direction of the border.

Even though I could see the older tracks, which were five to six days old the weather and ground temperature had started to cause them to deteriorate. Fortunately, the vegetation was still flagging[44] in the direction of their travel and I could see that they had made no attempt to mask their tracks. This meant that they were either confident of not being caught or they were unskilled in the art of tracking. This was a major bonus, even if they did try to hide their tracks, they would still leave signs of their movements and this would indicate to me their state of mind. If they were being cautious, it would show that they had a degree of awareness and therefore we needed to act with more caution.

I took measurements of the older tracks and based on their true track[45] I did a calculation which gave me an estimation as to the height[46] of my quarry. One person was approximately 6' 4", and the other was 5' 8". The border was two miles away; making our job that little bit more difficult because of the distance involved.

I decided not to hang around by looking at every single print, it would take too much time; exposing us to attack. We took in some water and had a couple of snack bars to help us work: the rest and play would come later. Studying the landscape as I ate, I took in every detail of the ground ahead by looking at the lay of the land. This would help me to work out their direction of travel over a longer distance; this is because the land can force people to go in a particular direction due to the path of least resistance. Animal trails could also be used for speed and ease of travel. I checked in with my team, briefing them on what I had found. We paused for a moment before moving off, this time allowed us to switch into a different state of mind; one of the hunter. The chances were that they had already crossed over the border long ago. Therefore, I did not consider it a hot pursuit[47], none the less we still needed to be alert.

***

The ground ahead was mostly uphill giving anyone watching us the advantage; like a game of chess we had to think several moves ahead. Where possible, we made maximum use of what cover was available. Even though we were moving uphill their stride was longer than I would have expected for the terrain we were in. I concluded that they were in a hurry to get back over the border, otherwise, their stride would have been shorter. The plan was not to directly follow their trail to the crossing point, doing so would give away the fact that we were onto them. We had to assume we were being watched, therefore we had to make it look like we were carrying out a routine patrol. This meant that we had to move away from the trail and re-join it further along.

While the dew was visible, we moved as fast as possible at one point their tracks headed into a boggy area. It was not long before I could no longer see their tracks; the ground quickly filled with water wherever we were stepping. It was clear that their tracks had disappeared as quickly as ours and in so doing it masked their direction of travel; any plants they stepped on would have rapidly sprung back up, as they did with us. In the distance I could see a large break in a hedgerow which marked the border between the north and the south, it was the only break too be seen. Their direction of travel indicated this is where they were heading. Again, we broke away from the trail.

Arriving at the bottom of the field, we swung left and headed back up the hill following the hedgerow until we came to the top of the ridge line where the large break was. I soon located and identified one of the target's prints. This was made easier by the fact that a chunk of rubber was missing from the right heel of his boot and also a nail was stuck in the tread, which showed up really well in the mud.

***

When tracking a group I look for a tread or a gait that stands out from all other tracks. To get an idea of how an individual moves I would walk alongside their trail mirroring their tracks: this lets me know if they have an injury or if they were carrying something heavy; like a weapon. It was clear to see from the tracks heading towards the cache, that one of individuals tracks showed a deeper imprint compared to the other persons, indicating he was indeed carrying something heavy.

Interestingly, footprints can give you more information than a fingerprint for example if someone tries to backtrack[48] by trying to place their feet exactly into their previous tracks it would show up. We are designed to move forward not backwards, therefore it is not possible to put your foot exactly into the same track. Another indicator is when moving forward we place the heal down first, this gives us an edge in the ground, as we move forward, we create an explosion of dirt. When moving backwards the edge shows up at the toe and the explosion is at the heel.

Their tracks would also show me if they were looking backwards indicating that they are making sure they were not being followed. I also made sure that I could identify the other person's tracks as well in case they split up or if one of the tracks had become fouled[49]. All this puts meat on the bone and helps me to understand my quarry. I was now feeling:

Calm, collected and on point...

Chapter 7

End of Mission

We went to ground on the ridgeline using the trees scattered along it as cover. Having identified that their crossing point was not in regular use, we lay there for a while before carrying on. The weather was starting to warm up. I was looking back in the direction of where the cache was, when I heard the sound of fingers clicking. I turned to see Jock indicating over the border. He was pointing into the valley below at a car which had just pulled into a lay-by.

I watched as four men got out of the car and walked into a small wood on our side of the road. I wondered if we were about to witness an ASU[50] crossing the border. They were not carrying any weapons, not that I could see; they may have been hidden in the woods for them to collect. A strong feeling percolated through my body in anticipation of a possible contact with the IRA as they crossed the border. The feeling I was experiencing was a mixture of fear and excitement. I whispered to my men to stay alert.

A short while later, only three men came out of the woods, they climbed into their car and drove off, they appeared to be in no rush. It was as if they felt confident that they would not be challenged. I can only guess what happened to the fourth man, perhaps he was a tout or someone who had crossed the line, and the IRA decided to put him to sleep if indeed it was the IRA. Soon after the Gardaí[51] arrived. They purposefully walked in the direction of the wood; returning ten minutes later, seemingly unfazed by what they had found. They then drove off and shortly after we headed towards our extraction point.

***

It was a hot day, and the horseflies were having a field day with us. We could not use insect repellent as the smell would compromise our position. We were well-hidden, I was so close to the road I could almost touch it. I was dying for a brew a nice cup of tea would go down a treat. Later that afternoon, a man walked up the road towards us. Again, we prepared for a possible contact, given that we were deep in IRA territory. He could have been a scout checking out the area for patrols. As he got closer to where I was, he slowed and stopped, turning to face my direction he moved even closer to me. My heart missed a beat for a moment I thought he had seen me.

All I could see was his boots and part of his legs through the large thick clumps of ferns and nettles that I was hiding under. Then I heard the familiar sound of a zip being undone; the next thing I knew he was pissing over me and to make matters worse he decided to write his name in the undergrowth with his urine. I could feel the warm liquid on my legs as it soaked through my combat trousers. I was not a happy teddy bear. It made the thought of extraction all the more attractive, along with a hot steamy shower.

As I grinned and bore it; the rest of the guys were looking at me with big smiles on their blacked-out faces. They were gesturing with their hands as if they were pulling on a cow's udder. I thought, you bastards take the piss why don't you. Still, I would have done the same had I been one of them. I so wanted to shout out and scare the crap out of this guy, stopping him in mid-flow and maybe in the process he would lag his trousers. But of course, I could not.

***

It was now day seven and it was time to head for our extraction point, which was about a mile away. Once in location Taff sent the codeword 'Triangle'.

Having dropped off another patrol a few miles away, the RAF then headed for our location arriving at the HLZ[52] on time. Flying low over the treetops, the pilot banked sharply and landed in the field to our front. We wasted no time, with our heads down we boarded the Lynx and strapped in. Peter was in position by the open door and ready to give covering fire if needed. The Heli lifted rapidly and banked sharply, giving us a good view of the ground directly below us. We watched as the forty shades of green that is Bandit Country disappeared from our view.

On our return to base my first IA[53] would normally be a brew and a fag (cigarette) before anything else. However, on this occasion, I changed it.

I could stay under this shower forever…

The Author

Geoffrey served in the Royal Regiment of Artillery for 22 years, retiring as a Staff Sergeant. A keen birder and conservationist. In 1993 the Queen awarded him the British Empire Medal (BEM) in the New Year's Honours for his services to Anglo-German Relations and Conservation.

He helped to established a Nature-reserve called the Zachariassee, in Germany which has been in existence for over 27 years. In 2008 Geoffrey completed a Master's (MSc) in Addiction Psychology and Counselling at London's Southbank University, his research was called 'Exploring How People with Addictions Experienced Nature-Awareness as a Therapeutic Intervention'.

He went on to develop his Nature Awareness activities into what is now known as Natural Awareness. Since then he has successfully worked with addictions, disaffected youth and others throughout the UK, Europe, and the USA.

He has illustrated bird books, breeding atlases and leaflets for rare birds as part of various worldwide bird conservation programmes.

He is the author of the Discover Nature Awareness (DNA) series and 'More Birds Than Bullets' - My Life with Birds.

Acknowledgements

I wish to express my gratitude and thanks to everyone who gave their permission to use their photographs and I am grateful to the unknown photographers. I thank those that helped with their advice: Jody Lapinskas, Garon Hawkes, Mark Davis, Stan Harper, Maurice Newall, Roy Grimes, Jim Hutton (RIP), Vicky Burke, Geoff Dunsmore, Barry Smale, Jamie Mc Creedy, Stephan Natynczuk, Tim Pearson, and Perry McGee.

Front/Back Cover: Geoffrey McMullan
Proof Reader: Rob Geary

Photographers:	Images	Page
Unknown:	Jim Hutton 40th Field Regiment R.A.	1
Unknown:	The Bone in Ardoyne, Belfast 77	21
David Lyons:	Farmland between Camlough Mountain and Newry, County Armagh.	21
Unknown:	Cache of weapons, Belfast 77	24
Unknown:	Mobile Patrol, Belfast 77	25
Unknown:	VCP, Belfast 77	31
Unknown:	Norman Harris, Belfast 77	39
Unknown:	Geoff Roberts, Queens Street	47
Unknown:	Myself on a rural patrol	50
Mick Kelly:	Northern Ireland	51
Mick Kelly:	Northern Ireland	57
Unknown:	Myself and Ian (Snake) Duff	60
Unknown:	Myself, Belfast 1977	61

Leaving a Review:

You can leave a review on Amazon, Goodreads, or any other book related website/blog. If you do not like writing reviews, you can still leave feedback by simply clicking the number of stars you feel the book is worth. All feedback is welcomed regardless of if it good, bad, or indifferent. It would be appreciated if you also sent a copy of your review to the author by e-mail: geoffrey@macmullan.plus.com

Customer Reviews

 38

4.8 out of 5 stars

5 star	██████████	87%
4 star	█	10%
3 star		3%
2 star		0%
1 star		0%

Pathfinder-UK Books
https://geoffreymcmullan.yolasite.com/

Discover Nature Awareness Series

DNA 1: Our Relationship with Nature
ISBN: 978-0-9576181-0-7 (In English)
ISBN: 978-0-9576181-7-6 (In German)
ISBN: 978-0-9576181-8-3 (In Spanish)
ISBN: 978-0-9576181-9-0 (In Italian)

DNA 2: Understanding Nature through Play
ISBN: 978-0-9576181-1-4

DNA 3: Exploring Bird Language
ISBN: 978-0-9576181-2-1

Website Link:
https://discovernatureawareness.yolasite.com/

More Birds Than Bullets - My Life with Birds
ISBN: 978-0-9576181-4-5

Website Link:
https://morebirdsthanbullets.yolasite.com/

www.ingramcontent.com/pod-product-compliance
Lightning Source LLC
Chambersburg PA
CBHW051958290426
44110CB00015B/2288